[redacted]

ECHOES OF CELTIC CHRISTIANITY

Timothy Pitt

illustrated by

Graeme Clark

British Library Cataloguing in Publication Data:
a catalogue record for this publication is available from the British Library

ISBN 978-1-912052-84-4

Typeset in 11.5pt Minion Pro at Haddington, Scotland

Printed by Books Line

Introduction

This book is dedicated to my wife, Elspeth, whom I love and treasure: my *Anam Cara* who stands with me and for me, who encourages and challenges me, who leads and guides and who puts up with my humour, actually laughing with me and not at me.

And to our two sons, Callum and Ewan, In gratitude for their grace when faced with yet another trip or half-told story.

With love, respect and gratitude to too many people to mention, so a representative few are: my brother and sister-in-law, Christopher and Judy (my round tower and high cross); Emma and Kevin Santry (cycling, coffee and Christian fellowship); Brian Hardin and SarahJane Morrone of the Daily Audio Bible (voices who became friends); Pastor Adam Stadtmiller of La Jolla Christian Fellowship, San Diego, USA (my non-brother brother); Penelope Warne of the law firm CMS (a modern day Hild); Graeme Clark (who landed in my email inbox one day and stunned me with his beautiful and atmospheric photographs) and Johnny and Kate Humphrey (walking with us on our faith journey in relationship).

Timothy Pitt

Foreword

There was a sweet spot in Elie behind the Golf Hotel where as a boy I discovered that if you cried out an echo would return with just enough delay to make it feel that it came from a different place. As Christians today cry out for answers amidst the crisis of church, climate and community echoes of the ancient Celtic saints speak to us from a different time and place of the power of prayer, the value of generous hospitality, of creative community and courageous discipleship and witness.

Graeme Clark

Contents

1 The Journey Begins

As a young boy I went on a day trip to Iona by ferry where memories of an imposing church building and a lot of walking – oh, and an eery stillness – were embodied. Here was a spiritual space that encouraged a lively seven year old to slow down, enjoy the peace and see everything in a bit more colour.

That 'thin place' experience of the divine stayed with me and over the years it started to shape my heart. I sensed I was being nudged in a particular direction. I knew almost instinctively that this was a mixture of the historical and the spiritual. I was looking at the Celtic culture as it merged into Anglo-Saxon attitudes. If I listened carefully, I could hear their voices calling and could see their pathways before me. But how could I start to learn? What resources or clues were there? Slowly, things started to fall into place.

I was at a Christian Conference and not sure which talk to attend. Down at the bottom of the conference agenda was a small entry for a series of talks throughout the week: Celtic Christian Traditions by Ray Simpson, the founding 'Guardian' of the International Community of Aidan and Hilda based on Lindisfarne. Aidan I had heard of, and knew to be of the Celtic Christian culture, but I was not quite sure what was linking him with Lindisfarne and this mysterious Hilda (or 'Hild' as I came to find her Anglo-Saxon name to be). I bought a recording of a longer series of talks by Ray. I started to notice Celtic Christian books in book shops, the odd one at a friend's house, a book received as a gift and some books which had recently been re-printed after a gap. A stack of books on the floor beside my favourite chair grew like a fast-motion stalagmite. But the books were not ignored. One by one, I opened them, I read them and I was drawn into the world of dynamic faith and vast imagination.

As the books opened up to me, so did the real world. When you start to look up and out, it's amazing how much is hidden in plain sight. I became a tourist on a mission – I suppose you could call me a pilgrim looking for a closeness with God in the locations, the high crosses and thin places of old. The Celts started to step into the sunlight and I found myself drinking in the connection, reflecting on the attraction and trying to analyse my reaction all at the same time. So I tried to take note of what I was learning, what I was hearing and who I was becoming.

I had time to reflect, time to contemplate and time to be shaped by these echoes of old.

Ask the former generation and find out what their ancestors learned. (Job 8:8)

2 Introducing the Celts

Celts are thought to have come from continental Europe, from around modern-day Marseille, first referred to as 'Keltoi' by the Greeks in 517BC with even Herodotus mentioned these Keltoi.

But a divergence occurred; a wandering of cousins.

The Continental Celts (primarily France and Iberia) could regard themselves as those who stayed close to home, and although Julius Caesar noted that they referred to themselves as Celts, they became known to all by their Roman name of Galli or Gauls.

A group of Celts – or Galli – journeyed east and south and in the 3rd century BC they had found both a new home and a new identity, settling in the central Turkish highlands which became known as Galatia. Paul wrote to the Galatians highlighting faith above (but not to the exclusion of) works; Celtic Christians in Britain and Ireland were led by their faith to act through hospitality and mission work. Tellingly, Paul wrote to the Galatians of life by the Spirit; the relationship with the Holy Spirit was significant to the Celtic Christians. They had freedom in going where the Holy Spirit led and they knew they could not capture or tame it – this found expression in the Celtic Christian imagery of pursuing the Holy Spirit as chasing the Wild Goose. As Paul wrote in Galatians 5:18: "But if you are led by the Spirit, you are not under the law."

The Insular Celts were those who migrated north. They were the Celts of Britain and Ireland and they came to southern Scotland which was then considered as far north as you could (safely) go. This was the land called Hen Ogledd or the 'old north.' These Celts painted their bodies and were known to the Greeks as 'Pretanoi' or 'painted ones.' Their lands were called 'Pretannia,' from which comes Britannia and the name for the whole British Isles; its people being the Britons.

The people living beyond them, in what is now central and northern Scotland, also painted their bodies. The Romans reached that far north and recorded them in AD297 as 'Picti' – Latin indicating painted or tattooed people. They were the Picts.

There is no clear record of how Celtic Christianity 'appeared.' Certainly, Aristobulus who died in AD99 was bishop of Britain, and St Ninian was a Briton who evangelised to the Picts from AD397, beginning from his base in Whithorn in south west Scotland.

Even as I was discovering who the Celtic Christians were as they grew and flourished, I was realising who they were not. This was not about nationality or nationalistic attitudes. This was a time when Edinburgh and the Lothians were in the English (Anglo-Saxon) kingdom of Northumbria; when Strathclyde was under Welsh influence; and when Dál Riata was the kingdom that combined part of Northern Ireland with the western coastline of Scotland (Argyll or 'Coast of the Gaels') and its islands, leaving the lands to the north for the Picts.

Celtic Christianity was not an established or institutional organisation, but an expression of Christianity through the culture of a people. And they seemed to be a true 'people' – not just a bunch of imposing men, for we see much female influence amongst the Celts. In Roman society, a woman was effectively her husband's property, without rights and unable to give lawful evidence. A Celtic woman continued to own anything she brought into the marriage and could be elected to leadership of her tribe or community. This system was possibly re-enforced by the strong community nature of Celtic life.

And it was not mere spirituality, following pagans and druids with their devotion to nature . . . and their human sacrifice. This was Christian spirituality: loving God the Father, Son and Holy Spirit, seeking to reflect the grace and compassion of Jesus and offering hospitality and love to all.

Celtic Christianity flourished but half a millennia later its decline was confirmed, rather than begun, by the Synod of Whitby in AD664. King Oswiu of Northumbria called the Synod, or conference, to hear the evidence and decide whether to follow the Augustinian (Roman) or Celtic expressions of Christianity. It was chaired by Hild who was the Abbess at Whitby. She led the entire community of nuns and monks at perhaps the most significant monastery of its day. She was responsible for faith, well-being and advancement as well as for the workers providing food and vellum (cow hide on which to transcribe copies of the Bible) and for the schools and hospitals. We will hear more of her later.

The decision went with Rome, and the Celtic Christian way of life was soon overwhelmed and obscured by the Church of Rome, but with a decidedly Anglo-Saxon spin. There were a few more conversations in history, a few more echoes marked out, but Celtic Christianity was never again as influential. I realised I was starting to look at the ending of a way of life although I had not yet really met the people themselves. I wanted to know more of what happened to Hild, or why Oswiu decided as he did. But I needed to know who these people were before I could find out what became of them.

> *May God Almighty bless you and make you fruitful and increase your numbers until you become a community of peoples. (Genesis 28:3)*

Hill Path

3 Equipped for the Journey

I had discovered an element of who the Celtic Christians were, of where they came from and where they lived. I had studied hard facts and looked at bare locations. I knew that they had been evangelised and had come to know the Lord. But they were still a disembodied people to me, calling out in only half-heard echoes. I realised I needed to find out what caused them to lead their lives the way they did. I needed to find out if they had a set of guiding principles that helped inform their interpretation of Mark 12:30-31, where Jesus said:

> *"Love the Lord your God with all your heart and with all your soul and with all your mind and with all your strength.' The second is this: 'Love your neighbour as yourself.' There is no commandment greater than these."*

What did this look like for them? How did they walk it out? I continued to immerse myself in the history and realised I would need to pull together the principles of who they were; of why they did what they did. Perhaps that would show what guided them in their life choices.

My intention now was to find out what the Celtic Christians held central to their lives as Christians, so that I could look out at the world from their perspective: see with their eyes, hear with their ears and perhaps draw closer to God as I adopted their heart attitude in worship.

I was getting closer to them, but they were still tantalisingly out of reach. I found myself chasing a different kind of wild goose, for even as I identified a trait or recurring idea, so another couple flitted in the shadows.

As I looked at aspects of life that defined Celtic Christianity, I became conscious that it was a holistic way of life. I could not isolate one aspect and declare that I then had the definitive answer to the question of who they were.

Looking at what they did and what was important to them, I settled on seven themes which to me made up the core essence of a Celtic Christian. This brought Celtic Christianity closer to me, because they were things I could do (or aspire to do). They were themes which would help me bring focus to the flickering images; would help me discern the echoes of their stories and lives. The themes were attractive; they were attainable – with self-discipline – and they were rewarding in their own right. But they were not an end-goal. Rather, they were both a series of actions and a presence of being that led towards something deeper. And they rested on four key concepts.

These concepts were an outpouring of their faith; the strength of their relationship. It seemed odd to be looking at concepts underpinning themes when the concepts were themselves an outpouring. But this made sense when I looked at it in terms of Celtic art: the intricate knotwork of an interlaced and unbroken cord. And so it was inevitable that as I groped my way along the concepts, I should find certain foundations woven in, supporting and yet leading.

Five foundations started to explain not just who they were, but what they did. They gave reason and purpose to the Celtic Christians. The echoes were becoming more distinct, clearer and insistent. The images were crystalising against a landscape that was coming into focus.

So I started with seven themes of Celtic Christianity, drilled down to four concepts of Celtic Christianity, rested on five foundations and emerged with one way of life. It was not about the different numbers involved – for others, there may be additional or alternative principles and elements that provide that necessary clarity. But the singular life was important, for it was a life given wholly to Jesus, enabling us to praise Jesus, to worship and adore and to continue our journey such that we are never alone; never lost in the darkness.

Blessed are those who have learned to acclaim you, who walk in the light of your presence, LORD. (Psalm 89:15)

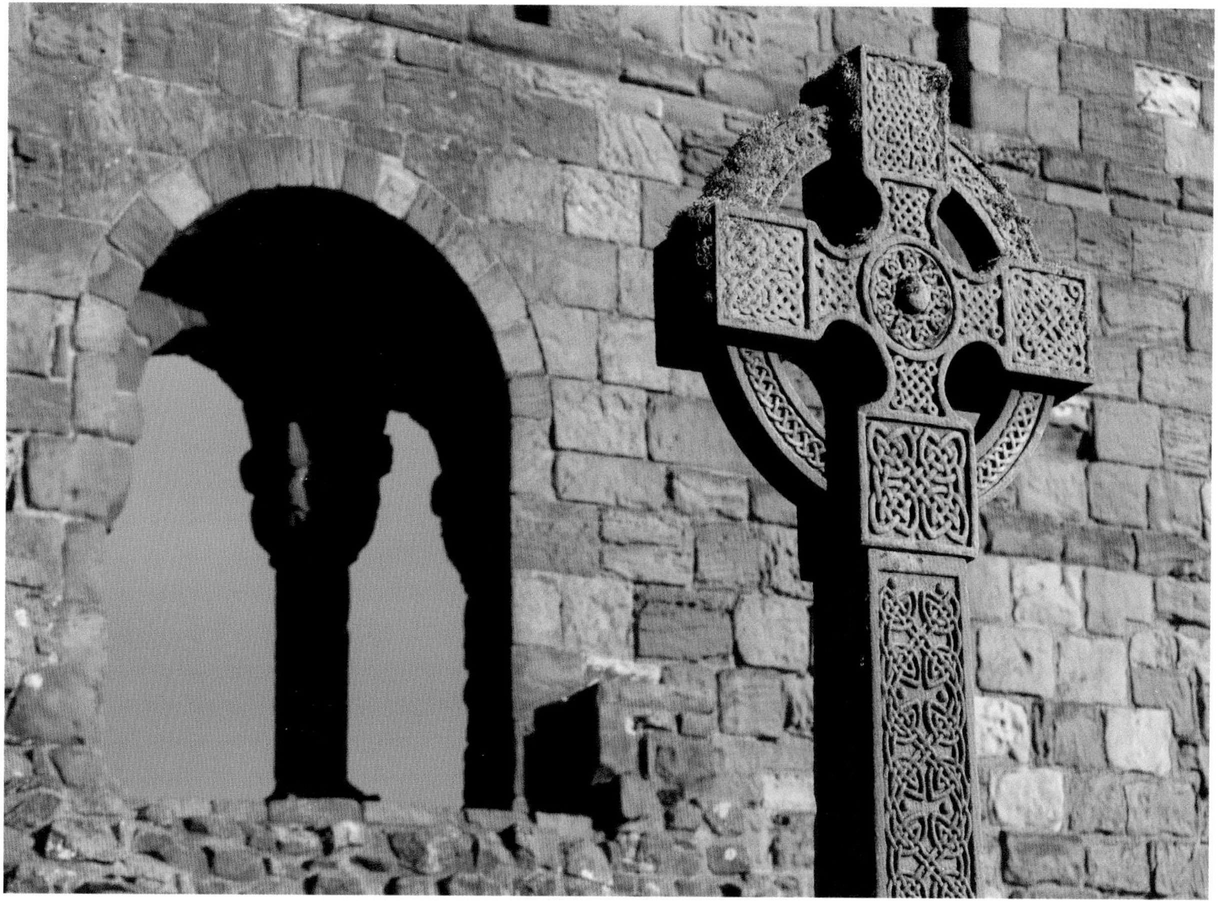

4 Themes and Concepts; Foundations and Rule

In looking at Celtic Christians life, seven ***themes*** emerged for me which interlink and provide mutual support.

Prayer. Celtic Christians loved God (Father, Son and Holy Spirit). They did not just want to know about Him, but wanted to be in relationship with Him. Prayer was their foundation, and led to everything else. They prayed for strength and protection; they prayed blessings on themselves and others. As children, we innocently ask our parents when we need or want something. We remain children of God, and whilst He has the advantage of knowing us and our needs better than we know ourselves, still:

> *'So I say to you: ask and it will be given to you; seek and you will find; knock and the door will be opened to you. For everyone who asks receives; the one who seeks finds; and to the one who knocks, the door will be opened. 'Which of you fathers, if your son asks for a fish, will give him a snake instead? Or if he asks for an egg, will give him a scorpion? If you then, though you are evil, know how to give good gifts to your children, how much more will your Father in heaven give the Holy Spirit to those who ask him!' (Luke 11: 9-13)*

This inspiration was drawn straight from . . .

Scripture. For Celtic Christians, the Bible was their encyclopaedia, history book, guide to healthy living and source of future planning. It was their route map to a closer relationship to God. They were especially drawn to the Psalms, taking them as personal prayers. They carved Scripture scenes on Tall Crosses. Those who could read would read to others, for they lived in . . .

Community. They lived by supporting each other, both in mission and basic hospitality. Even hermits would not be in total seclusion, for they would meet in fellowship and share, enjoying having . . .

Soul Friendship. They discussed their lives with their Anam Cara (or 'soul friend'), not necessarily looking for advice, but holding themselves accountable. This was a vital relationship for

Celtic Christians. Brigid, well respected in her leadership role as Kildare Abbess, reportedly said, 'Not having a soul friend is like not having a head.' Anam Cara was both Christian mentor and confidante: we should find our own today, for together they would consider their thoughts and actions and, in transparency, would be in . . .

Contemplation. They spent time thinking, not just aimlessly drifting from one task or snatching at the next. A modern contemplation would be 'What Would Jesus Do' and they could consider this anywhere and at any time. Any activity could be an act of worship, being their . . .

Pilgrimage. They did not have to travel (although they travelled extensively). They did not have to find a Thin Place (although that helped give them focus and enabled them easily to meet with God). A prayer walk was pilgrimage; providing hospitality was pilgrimage. They did not have to go anywhere on pilgrimage (although many did) because Jesus is their, and our, Emmanuel: God *with* us. They just needed to set regular time consciously to be with God; to find their . . .

Rhythm. The Celtic Christians sought regularity and rhythm, progress and balance. Through the rhythm of the seasons they could witness God who creates; through the rhythm of rest they could benefit from God who blesses.

Seven themes. The Celtic Christians did not have the perfection of Jesus. But they sought it; they sought God and were with God. And the number seven in the Bible symbolises completion and perfection.

> *And the words of the Lord are flawless, like silver purified in a crucible, like gold refined seven times. (Psalm 12:6)*

Those seven themes enabled Celtic Christianity to express itself through four clear ***concepts***, being:

Prayer retreats. Woven into the 'Thin Places' where the Celts found it easy to connect with God, sensing the Holy Spirit. We will look at some Thin Places later, remembering that Celtic Christians saw everything as a basis for prayer, not just a specific hill top. A countryside walk could be a prayer retreat, as could time spent weaving. Viewed with modern eyes, Celtic Christians are sometimes accused of godly superstition - instead of saying 'touch wood' or whatever, they would continuously invoke God's blessing. Quite simply, they just saw God working in everything, which gave them cause to pause, wonder in awe and worship God.

Mission work. As well as evangelising to Celts, Picts and other Britons, they undertook plenty of basic and local mission work. They were called to provide for the poor of their own community and simply to 'be there' for others - a visible and reassuring Christian presence.

Hospitality. Celtic Christians were famed for hospitality. So too are many peoples around the world, but it is notable that the Scottish Clan system, which indirectly grew out of Celtic society, held hospitality almost as a necessity.

Martyrdom. Some Celtic Christians were led (or driven) to extremes and indeed the so-called 'Three Martyrdoms' became famous, encompassing red martyrs who died for their faith (not necessarily actively pursuing their own deaths!); blue martyrs who lived as hermits (only a minority of Celtic Christians; perhaps gaining fame in part because they were a minority); and white martyrs who were missionaries (all were called to be missionaries whether travelling or staying at home). Yet I saw a fourth element of martyrdom at play in the Celtic Christian world. It was a subtle and often unremarked-upon martyrdom, but one which clearly looked to Jesus as the exemplar and model. It was simply martyrdom to self in the sense of putting others first, of seeking to serve others. This shaped and informed their acts of hospitality, their outreach to others in mission work, and their sense of serving in community.

Those seven principles rested on the four concepts and they in turn were shaped and polished by five clear ***foundations***:

- A strong evangelical love for the Bible;
- A deep spiritual life;
- A respectful commitment to the poor;
- A sustaining commitment to God's creation;
- A charismatic life.

The reality was not a romantic idyll of perfection. Even those who held to the concepts and foundations would fail, hurt others, surrender to temptations and display inhumanity to each other. But, by and large, they knew the Scripture, they prayed and sought God, they looked to carry out Jesus' teaching, they cared for God's creation as stewards and they shared God's love. We can learn from that today.

The Rule. Even for the Celtic Christians at the time, it seemed that a formalised Celtic Christian society was hard to define, replicate and grow as there was no set teaching or standard of practising these concepts; each community had its own way or 'Rule' of Life. This stemmed from the Columbian Celtic Tradition with its commitment to a common Rule, and this Rule of life and witness bound the Celtic Christian community to God and each other. It wove together all they did within the seven themes, all they rested on in the four concepts and all that shaped them through the five foundations. As such, their Rule of Life enabled the Celtic Christians to attune to

God's desires for them, to align with Jesus' walk with them, and to be sustained by the Holy Spirit leading them.

A Rule is not regulation but rhythm. It supports our changing needs as we grow in faith and allows us to work with the seasons in which we live. What the Celtic Christians did – and what we can seek to do – is to find our rhythm of life in God; not work against it or even drive on relentlessly pursuing, for there is much to be gained from including a season of rest.

In practice this addresses both the positive and negative. It positively leans into godly habits and practices, drawing us closer to God and enabling us to have time with God. Remember that for Celtic Christians, any activity could be worship – they reshaped the routine of walking into the relationship of a prayer-walk. It is also helps avoid evil and negativity: identifying and helping us remove habits and practices which prevent us from consciously being with God, consciously doing what He calls us to do.

It is called a 'Rule' but it is not a legalistic set of requirements. The word comes from the Latin for 'trellis'. The Rule is a framework to lift us up in Jesus, enabling better growth and preventing an attack of disease from below.

An example of a Rule in the Celtic tradition is found in the Iona community's commitment:

Daily prayer, worship with others and regular engagement with the Bible and other material which nourishes us.

Working for justice and peace, wholeness and reconciliation in our localities, society and the whole creation.

Supporting one another in prayer and by meeting, communicating, and accounting with one another for the use of our gifts, money and time, our use of the earth's resources.

Sharing in the corporate life and organisation of the Community.

And ultimately, this comes from love.

And now these three remain: faith, hope and love. But the greatest of these is love. (1 Corinthians 13:13)

5 The Landscape of the Journey

I had found myself amongst the shadows that echoed, doing what they did and using what they used. I understood that regular reading of Scripture, truly contemplating it and finding a rhythm amongst my own community did help me to draw closer to God. It could still be an effort to quieten down, to see the peace and make the pilgrimage, but I found I was being richly rewarded by my efforts to offer up hospitality and being vulnerable enough to be accountable. It was not supposed to be like that – to be all about what I got out of it. It was supposed to be offering care and support to others for their benefit, not my own.

And yet the more I practiced it, the calmer I was, with less worry and more fulfilment. I had a Celtic Christian tool box, and a context in which to operate. But still there was something lacking; I wasn't quite there yet.

I turned that phrase around and around as I gazed at it and into it. I wasn't 'there.' Was there somewhere else I ought to be?

It was the backdrop; the place. And yet it was simply being. Anywhere became any-when; nowhere became now and here.

I wanted to follow the Celtic Christians back into the past, and I realised that I needed to know where they were; I needed to see their favourite places, whether that was the countryside or somewhere in their heart. I needed guidance – waypoints to the past and encouragement on the journey. And I needed to rest in the presence of the Lord.

In fact, and as the Celtic Christians had done so many years before me, I needed to reach out to God. As I did, I would find that He had already reached to me. I could not picture it, but I knew it would an entrancing place where I met with God; it would be a special and holy place and yet an ordinary place. It would be a Thin Place.

A Thin Place is a place where God appears closer – where there is a mere veil between earth and heaven; between physical and spiritual. It is not simply the historical place where something happened to someone else long ago, but can include places of seclusion and places of activity.

Celtic Christians spent time with God in Thin Places, in worship and wonder.

Historical places can be important. Stop and pause for a moment: Moses saw the burning bush. “Do not come any closer,” God said. “Take off your sandals, for the place where you are standing is holy ground.” (Exodus 3:5) How would you react today if you travelled there stood at that very spot? Or if you were walking up the now archaeologically-investigated steps leading to Caiaphas’ Palace, the route Jesus was led after his initial questioning by Annas? Might such a place give you pause to think, to consider what has gone before and to contemplate God’s presence in all history?

Secluded places can assist our devotional time. The so-called Desert Mothers and Desert Fathers were hermits who lived mainly in the Scetes desert in Egypt from around AD250 onwards. They sought a place where they could be at peace, undistracted, with God. As Celtic Christianity took hold and flourished, many found inspiration in the same life. Dysart is a place in Fife, Scotland, and the name comes from the Gaelic word *dìseart* meaning hermitage, which itself comes from the Latin *desertum* or desert. St Serf lived at Dysart for a while – we shall hear more of him.

But a thin place was not necessarily for one person alone. Iona is possibly the most famous “Thin Place’ in the world. Columba and 12 fellow monks arrived there in AD565 and eventually there came to be a community of some hundreds. Clonfert grew to be a community of some 3,000 brothers and at Whitby, Hild was in charge of a combined order (male and female) of many thousands, including those who looked after the cattle (it would take about 170 calves to produce enough vellum for a single Bible) and the other animals as well as those tending the fields for crops to feed both the people and the animals. A hive of activity and yet a place of peaceful encounter with God’s spirit.

Many places became known for their ‘thin’ atmosphere in earliest times (again, Iona is a good example); some (such as Inchcolm Island, the so-called ‘Iona of the East’ in the Firth of Forth) were founded much later but retain their 'thin' characteristic. Others developed Christian affiliations much later still, but are coming into their own (worship services were only held at Sannox, on the Isle of Arran, from the mid-18th century, but it has that thin quality and is now being redeveloped into a Christian retreat modelled on the Celtic Christian way).

A word for Iona? Tranquil. Incholm would be peaceful and Sannox restful. Lindisfarne, the Holy Island is breathtaking. But it is not *them*. The most important aspect of a 'Thin Place' is discernible when you remember one of the key principles held by the Celtic Christians. They were followers of Jesus and they knew Him as Immanuel – God with us. In other words, the most important element was not the special hill or the amazing view. It was being alert and attentive to God in all places, for He is with us always.

Then the LORD said, "Go out and stand on the mountain before the LORD. Behold, the LORD is about to pass by." And a great and mighty wind tore into the mountains and shattered the rocks before the LORD, but the LORD was not in the wind. After the wind there was an earthquake, but the LORD was not in the earthquake. After the earthquake there was a fire, but the LORD was not in the fire. And after the fire came a still, small voice. (1 Kings 19:11-12)

6 Thin Places and Tall Crosses

Iona

Iona is a small island off Mull (which itself is off Oban in the West of Scotland), not quite 3 ½ square miles. Today, the only motorised vehicles allowed are those of the permanent residents. When Columba arrived in AD563, Iona formed a centre point for the loose Gaelic kingdom of Dál Riata, composed of the north of Ireland to the west and the Hebrides and Argyll to the east. It retained a spiritual prominence, but Dunkeld became politically and geographically more central to the church from cAD850 when the nation of Scotland was more or less established, losing Northern Ireland in the west but gaining more of mainland Scotland to the east.

Originally the monastery buildings were wattle and timber and only the ditch and earth bank remain from Columba's time. Around AD800 a stone chapel was built and this was enlarged over the years, becoming a full abbey producing Christian texts (including, seemingly, the Book of Kells) and manuscript Bibles as part of the monks' work amidst their daily rhythm of prayer and worship, work and rest.

After Rome's victory at the Synod of Whitby, the monks at Iona continued to hold onto strands of Celtic Christian ways, but first Augustinian ideas grew increasingly dominant and then, by 1200, the monastery had officially become Benedictine. It suffered various Viking raids (63 monks killed in one raid alone in AD806), was actually annexed to Norway by Magnus Barelegs and only returned in 1266. By then, Iona had established a spiritual importance throughout western Europe. Some 48 Scottish kings (including Macbeth) and queens, as well as Norwegian, English, Irish and French monarchs, are buried on Iona; their funeral processions would traverse the Street of the Dead, a medieval paved road leading from Abbey to graveyard, that still exists.

The abbey continued, with occasional alterations and rebuilding, until the Scottish reformation of 1560 when it was finally abandoned and fell into ruin. The 8th Duke of Argyll made safe the ruins and, in 1899, handed them over to the Iona Cathedral Trust to progress his rebuilding dream. From 1938 the Iona Community carried out extensive works and what began as an ecumenical social and evangelical campaign became a long term project with the building complex finally handed on to Historic Scotland in 2000 complete apart from the "next thing to do" that can always be found in addition to general maintenance.

So those are some of the hard facts, but what about the place itself – is it truly 'thin'?

It is. There is a sense of tranquillity over the whole island which seems to centre on the Abbey complex. The grass is a shade greener; the quiet is a tone quieter. When I was last there, I found that wherever I was – sitting in the Abbey pews or standing on the grassy hill outside, I just wanted to acknowledge God's majesty, to shelter in Jesus' power and to lean into the Holy Spirit's gentleness.

Is there a reason for that? I don't know. Perhaps so many people declare the place to be 'thin' that we arrive with the *expectation* of meeting easily with God.

And that is what we should carry on our travels physical and spiritual: an expectation of meeting easily with God, of connecting with His majesty, His power, His gentleness.

". . . live each day with holy awe and reverence throughout your time on earth." (1 Peter 1:17 – The Passion Translation)

Inchcolm Island

Columba is recorded as having visited Inchcolm (the "Iona of the East") in AD567, just a few years after founding his community on Iona. Inchcolm is a small island only six miles from Edinburgh city centre. But as with the way of Celtic Christians, we should remember that every journey, whatever length, can be a pilgrimage.

It is a way-point on the old ferry route from Edinburgh and the Lothians to Fife – there would have been a fleet of ferries along the coast, not just at South and North Queensferry, named for Queen Margaret, wife of King Malcolm Canmore. One of their sons, King Alexander I, took refuge on the island whilst attempting a crossing in stormy weather. He was sheltered by a Christian hermit at his *dìseart,* and in gratitude Alexander vowed to build an Augustinian monastery there.

Alexander died and the responsibility for completing the work was left to his brother, King David I. It became a full abbey in 1235 during the reign of Alexander II (and his queen, Marie de Coucy), David's grandson. The abbey was abandoned after the Scottish Reformation in 1560 and although it fell into ruin it was not the target for repeated attacks and total destruction. The result is the best preserved medieval abbey in Scotland (Pluscarden and Iona Abbeys having both been 'restored', not simply 'preserved').

But where does the Celtic Christianity element fit in? Remember, we are looking at a way of life, a culture of some of God's people and a thin place where we can meet with God. Visiting Inchcolm Island, I gained a sense of peace, of yearning for God. Edinburgh can be seen so close and clear, but at the same time it feels a world away.

I sensed the transition from the rhythm of the Celtic Christians to the foundations of the Augustinians. The cloisters inspire security in God. The magnificent octagonal Chapter House (meeting room) inspires orderliness in working for God. There is a quote from St Augustine on display: *"Dwell in the house with oneness of spirit, and let your hearts and minds be one in God."*

And that is the point: Dwell in the house, yes. Come to the thin place, sure. But do so in unity with your brothers and sisters, seeking together the Holy Spirit (chasing the Wild Goose). And, body and soul, be one in God. It's not the buildings or the Thin Place itself – it is our attitude to God; our choice to seek Him and worship Him.

I felt blessed praying on Inchcolm Island. As if to confirm the blessing, on the return trip I noticed the boat's commissioning prayer, framed and displayed, including:

"Lord . . .

You were with the Celtic monks who went out in small boats from Iona

To take the word of your evangel to the people of Scotland . . .

May those who travel on this boat and walk through the sacred ruins

Feel something of Your presence . . .

Touch their hearts so that their journey by this ship

May become a pilgrimage and that they return to the shore

More aware of the wonder of Your goodness and more committed

To seeking You and serving You all the days of their life . . ."

It is a prayer for us all.

The LORD protects and preserves them – they are counted among the blessed in the land – he does not give them over to the desire of their foes. (Psalm 41:2)

Sannox

Sannox (the Norse '*Sandvik*' means 'Sandy Bay') is a small village on the northeast coast of the Isle of Arran. This island has a tale to tell from earlier days. In the west is *Tobair Challumchille* (the 'spring of Columba') from where it is claimed Columba, looking up and realising he could still see Ireland, continued his White Martyr journey, ultimately arriving on Iona.

At Sannox, though, a chapel dedicated to the Archangel Michael was established around the 14th century – such association often denotes a spiritually significant place and a struggle. By 1800, the moderatist tradition was well-established – where enthusiasm was frowned upon and cold, formal worship was re-enforced by 'reason' (amidst a general acknowledgement that dark spirits held sway on the island). A struggle, indeed.

Into this culture, two evangelising ministers came to the island in 1800. Local landowners told several tenant farmers to leave the evangelists or leave their farms. They chose to leave their farms. They gathered at Sannox, and amazingly received offers of farm-holdings there. Initially 14 people, this became a congregation of 60 within 2 years, and in 1806 Alexander Mackay was appointed minister. Two early members were Duncan and Katherine Macmillan whose great grandson, Harold, became British Prime Minister in 1957.

In 1821 both land and permission were obtained for a church to be built instead of holding open-air services throughout the year. It opened in 1822 but only seven years later the population was much reduced amidst the Highland Clearances. The emigrants sailed to Canada where they built a replica church.

At Sannox, the church continued, led by Alexander Mackay until his death in 1856, after fifty years as minister there. The last permanent minister died in 1966, and by 1976 only occasional services were held with the building becoming dilapidated.

But the call of the Thin Place was heard, and the Sannox Christian Centre ('SCC') trust was established to redevelop the site as a house of prayer; a place of rest and restoration; and a site reflecting the Celtic Christian Mission of Christ at the centre, open to all.

The nearby cottage has been redeveloped into accommodation and the church is being restored, the overall site enhanced with further accommodation representing the *cave* (for our personal journey with God), a *common table* (God's provision of sustenance for all) next to a *road* (our godly outreach to others). And all this is around a focal-point Celtic cross.

I have stayed, prayed and worshipped there. For a place that has seen so much struggle, it surely is a place of spiritual significance. It is just so peaceful. It is as if you arrive to find God welcoming you, saying, "Relax! Take your time – settle in. When you are ready, come and let me know what's on your mind, what's on your heart. You are here; I choose to be here for you."

SCC has been guided by Isaiah 56:7, which is an appropriate verse for all Thin Places when we gather there.

These I will bring to my holy mountain and give them joy in my house of prayer. Their burnt offerings and sacrifices will be accepted on my altar; for my house will be called a house of prayer for all nations. (Isaiah 56:7)

Tall Crosses

We have seen that 'thin places' were places where people could more easily sense and acknowledge God's presence. They were not just a location, but were an expression of Christ in the lives of people at the time. Into that expression were planted huge symbols of the power and enigma of Celtic Christianity.

Tall Crosses are iconic of the Celtic Christian heritage and are powerful when set in the landscape of a Thin Place. But what were they for?

First, what are they? Carved from one piece of stone (usually granite or sandstone), they have a circle (nimbus) at the intersection. Most are intricately carved – often with specific scenes as well as with the *triqueta* or 3-cornered 'knot.' This knot, without start or end, symbolises the eternal Three-in-One: Father, Son and Holy Spirit. In some examples, carved scenes and knots appear to have been painted for added effect.

Heights average around 2 metres (6 ½ feet), but Monasterboice's Tall Cross in Ireland stands 6.5 metres (21 feet).

As to the nimbus, one theory is that the *cross* of Christ's suffering for our sins is made complete by the *halo* of His redemption for us. Another theory is that it was simply a practical means to support the weight of the arms of the cross. Both are correct, but neither is necessarily the single, overriding reason.

As to their purpose, rather than look back at what might have been, let us look from the perspective of a Celtic Christian at the time. What would they see? What was the context?

Villages were smaller, fewer and farther apart. They were reached along roads that were just worn tracks, lit only by daylight or moonlight in a less-farmed countryside of natural woodland and wild scrubland. The population was smaller, more were illiterate with few having access to the Bible or other books. But they travelled. And they still needed learning, direction and encouragement. Into this setting we place our Celtic Christian for whom everything could be a pilgrimage, a spiritual journey and an opportunity to contemplate God.

Jesus answered, "I am the way and the truth and the life. No one comes to the Father except through me. (John 14:6)

Tall Celtic crosses could be seen from afar; reassuring direction posts confirming that a traveller was on the right path to their destination: early march-stones and Google Maps way points.

Carved Celtic crosses were references for preaching. Local or travelling monks, nuns or leaders (or simply someone from the area) would preach beside the cross, illustrating their points with the carved scenes. Even a solo traveller could pause at a cross and learn from the picture narratives. Individual Celtic crosses were erected in memory of Disciples or particular saints, such as St. Mathew's Cross and St. Martin's Cross, both on Iona. The Celtic Christians (and those who came after) would have had constant encouragement.

Therefore, since we are surrounded by such a great cloud of witnesses, let us throw off everything that hinders and the sin that so easily entangles. (Hebrews 12:1)

We are more mobile now, and tend to use church buildings and internet, rather than a large stone cross outdoors, for preaching, direction-finding and remembering the examples of others. Rather than being *anchored to* our faith, we can be *led by* our faith as the Celtic Christians were. Perhaps we carry around a modern Celtic cross necklace or T-shirt logo. Let it not just be a pretty design, but a catalyst to remind ourselves of God's power and grace.

Pay attention to these stones. Whether you hear the message or read it, there is much for us to learn.

And Joshua recorded these things in the Book of the Law of God. Then he took a large stone and set it up there under the oak near the holy place of the Lord. (Joshua 24:26)

7 Journey into the Mist

Even as the Celtic Christians came into view in their own landscape, the history books record that they basically disappeared until aspects of their style and culture were recreated or re-invented for the late Victorian romantic idyll and onwards to the present day.

I thought of haar and wondered if the Celtic Christians had simply walked into the mist.

A haar is a sea fog. It is most often found on the east coast of Northumbria and Scotland. Although a dense, cold mist, it is found in the early mornings from April until September, and it burns off, usually to be replaced by bright and warming sunshine.

As they walked into the mist, they faded away until all we could hear was their voices, softer and fainter and leaving behind just the trace of an echo. Was that the echo that I had heard and which was now driving me on to find out about them?

I needed to follow the echoes, to draw close to them and hear them first-hand and build up a picture of the Celtic Christians.

Celtic Christianity was a way of life, familiar and embedded in the culture whereas the Church in Rome had a systematic approach to its own identity and workings; efficiency and uniformity.

Perhaps Celtic Christianity had found a way to walk with Jesus whereas Rome had found a way to walk for Jesus. The Celts looked to the individual – each person, each community. Rome found its cultural identity in the state: one in, all in. Faith led Celtic Christianity; faith anchored Rome.

I looked back at the narrative of Celtic History and saw that the decision of the Synod of Whitby was the defining point. King Oswiu had inherited the throne from his great and sainted brother, Oswald. Both had been raised in exile at Iona and followed the Celtic Christian way whereas Oswiu's wife, Queen Eanflæd, was from Kent and followed the Church in Rome.

When King Oswiu called a Synod in AD664, it was held under one of the most noble, significant and intellectual leaders of the day – Hild. And it was not held at the royal residences of Ad Gefrin or Bamburgh Castle, but at Hild's monastic community of Whitby (known, in pre-Viking times, as Streanæshealh): a holy place for a holy task. Wilfred used his knowledge and connections to plot and argue in favour of Rome. Colmán stood on his principles and stated them matter of factly. Hild moderated the meeting graciously, without favour to her own Celtic Christian upbringing and all the while, Oswiu listened and considered whilst no doubt Eanflæd influenced. The decision went the way of Rome and at that moment the Celtic Christian way of life walked off into the haar.

Hild accepted the final decision and continued worshiping God, leading her community and caring for the people. But Colmán with most of the Celts and 30 English monks from Lindisfarne, immediately left the Synod for Iona. Their replacements were from an Ireland that, in the main, already accepted Rome. Those who left continued the Celtic Christian ways, but by 716 even Iona accepted the Roman Order.

The conclusion of the Synod at Whitby perhaps simply reflected that the tide of advancing culture was already pushing the Celts away; that the circumstances of the day were calling for the uniformity of the Roman Church.

But the haar burns off to reveal a glorious and warm sunny outlook. if I could distil the essence of their godly lives within those Celtic Christian saints of old, would I reveal a glorious picture? Would I, in fact, uncover Jesus as the Celtic Christians saw Him?

Now I could look for them in the mist, one by one I could hear clearly what they were saying today and then I would witness not just the sustaining power of the sun on them, but the saving of the Son in them.

> *Jesus answered, "I am the way and the truth and the life. No one comes to the Father except through me. If you really know me, you will know my Father as well. From now on, you do know him and have seen him."* *(John 14:6-7)*

8 The Haar Burned Clear

I had seen the Celtic Christian way of life slip off into the mist. But I could hear them and identify what they stood for; who – together in fellowship – they represented.

I found much to contemplate in these people from the past and their attributes. Perhaps Wilfred was scheming, but he was also determined. Colmán was clearly principled. Hild was wise, generous, accommodating … in short, she had a noble quality of leadership. Celtic Christians often summarised their saints in this way to remember the individual, learn from them and promote aspects of the Christian faith to which all should aspire. A Celtic Christian 'saint' was simply a wise or inspiring individual from whom all can learn, not necessarily as consecrated by Rome.

I began to know and identify the saints and as I spent time with a number of them, I did start to see a picture of Jesus. We can focus just a little bit too much on one person or one trait, but when we step back, we start to see an image of Christ emerge. This what the echoes were saying: look to Jesus; see that reflection of perfection which, by grace, has been granted to each of us.

I looked for Jesus in the saints. I found descriptions of them that painted more colour into His name. I understood more of how the Celtic Christian saints expressed themselves – their prayers as an outpouring of their prayer hearts, their literature as an outpouring of their thoughts. Looking at the characteristics of some of the saints, I found a word or short phrase of description and put them together to build a picture of Jesus; a picture that is of Celtic Christians and is for us. It is a picture of Jesus for us to live by. It is not nearly complete, but still it's a start.

Ninian (Missional)

> *I, even I, have spoken; yes, I have called him. I will bring him and he will succeed in his mission. (Isaiah 48:15)*

Ninian's mission was to take the gospel to the southern Picts. He began this in AD397 from Whithorn, at the southern point of Galloway in Scotland. Basically, find Wigtown then head south, stopping before your feet get wet. Ninian was a Briton who followed Celtic Christianity and apparently studied in Rome – an attractive proposition for the Roman Christians after the Synod of Whitby and they made much of his great missional example.

Whithorn itself is known as the Cradle of Christianity in Scotland and hosts the oldest surviving Christian memorial in Scotland, the 5th century Latinus Stone which is inscribed: "We praise you, Lord" and declares that it was erected 'by Latinus aged 35 and his daughter aged 4.'

Like that stone, Ninian wanted firm foundations and a beacon of hope for his missional calling. At Whithorn he established a church of whitewashed stone, called the Candida Casa, or 'White House' (hence Whit … Horn). From there, he travelled widely, evangelising to, and converting, the southern Picts. He certainly reached Abercorn in West Lothian where, nearly 300 years later, Trumwine was based as Bishop of the Picts.

He achieved results, but later many Picts and Celts fell back into paganism. Patrick, writing some 50 – 75 years afterwards, referred to the 'Apostate Picts' Who had fallen back. Ninian was a pioneering missional who knew the risks. The success of pioneering mission may be precisely that it is pioneering: it is first where before was nothing; growth comes later.

Ninian pursued his mission, answering his calling to walk and work amongst the southern Picts. Early maps were shown on their side, not necessarily north-south, and Ninian's mission essentially took him across the land and up the East Coast. A missional trail can reasonably be plotted by noting the dedications to St Ninian around the country. They are found throughout the Pictish lands south of the Firths of Clyde and Forth, and around Stirling, Perth, Fife, Dundee and even up to Forfar. But the Highlands and Isles do not host sites of dedication to him.

Ninian died and was buried at Whithorn which became a place of pilgrimage. Robert the Bruce (1274 – 1329) travelled there to pray in his last days. James IV (1473 – 1513) walked 8 days on pilgrimage to Ninian's tomb, and links are being investigated of King Richard III of England (1452 – 1485) with Whithorn through his apparent pilgrimage there.

Ninian's life pointed to Jesus: discern your mission, as directed by God, with the success of your endeavours felt, in gratitude, many years later. God prepared Ninian; and then invited him to act.

Serf (Teaching)

> *Teach them his decrees and instructions and show them the way they are to love and how they are to behave. (Exodus 18:20)*

Serf, short for 'Servanus', lived from about AD485 to AD550. He appears to have come from Canaan and travelled to Rome where some records note him as having been elected Pope and serving for 7 years. At that time popes did not necessarily serve until death (an option recently revived!). His term of office coincided with an upturn in theological study and teaching.

Serf can then be traced journeying through Europe before arriving in what was to become Scotland. Like many Celtic Christians, he sought a place of seclusion where, free of distraction, he could be at peace with God, modelling this on the Desert Mothers and Fathers of the Scetes Desert. When Serf came to the Fife coast, he established a retreat at what is now the town of Dysart.

Eventually Serf moved on and founded a monastic establishment on an island (now known as St Serf's Inch) in Loch Leven, from where he evangelised and taught the surrounding Picts, taking forward some of Ninian's earlier missional work. Serf seems to have lived in rhythm, again reaching 7 years, the Biblical number of completion, before moving on. His settlement had long-since disappeared when David I founded an Augustinian priory on St Serf's Inch in 1150. After Serf left the island, he came to Culross where he established a place of holy education: monastery and school. He was leader of this Culross community when, in 528, a coracle came ashore, having started its journey on the Edinburgh side of the Forth, carrying the fleeing and heavily pregnant Princess Teneu. After landing at Culross, Teneu gave birth to a boy. St Serf took in both mother and son and oversaw the boy's education.

Taking this knowledge – both self-taught and apparently gleaned from his fruitful time in Rome – Serf could have stepped straight out of 2 Timothy, for it was of great significance that he was led to show compassion to Teneu when she was washed ashore, and then to teach her son:

> *What you heard from me, keep as the pattern of sound teaching, with faith and love in Christ Jesus. Guard the good deposit that was entrusted to you—guard it with the help of the Holy Spirit who lives in us. (2 Timothy 1: 13-14)*

Serf learned about God; he *knew* God. He studied, contemplated and walked with God – and he taught what he knew, not keeping it as 'secret knowledge' but seeing his very relationship with God as something to teach, to show and thus to inspire others. You do not need a classroom setting or a church pulpit to teach like this; you just need a willingness to walk with God, find His joy and be vulnerable enough to share it with others.

Kentigern (Preaching

> *Surely you remember, brothers and sisters, our toil and hardship; we worked night and day in order not to be a burden to anyone while we preached the gospel of God to you. (1 Thessalonians 2:9)*

Kentigern lived about AD528 – AD603, born in Culross in Fife, where his mother, Teneu, princess of Lothian, had fled. (Lothian was named after her grandfather Lleuddun.) Some tell of her love affair with Urien of Cumbria; others that he had assaulted her. Either way, unmarried, she fell pregnant and her father sought her death at Traprain Law. Her executioners were to stone her, but instead tied her to a cart and pushed it down the steep hill. Somehow she survived and escaped (some stories speak of help from her would-be executioners who were unnerved by her survival). From the shore of the Forth, she fled in a coracle across the water and was eventually found by Serf at Culross.

Kentigern was born and Serf cared for them both at his monastic school in Culross. He taught Kentigern and trained him as a priest, giving him the nickname Mungo ('dear friend'). Entering adulthood, Kentigern left and came to what is now Stirlingshire, stumbling upon the *dìseart* of a dying monk named Fergus. Kentigern stayed, praying with Fergus, who asked that Kentigern arrange his funeral. When the old man died, Kentigern put the body on a cart strapped to two oxen and asked God to show him an appropriate place. The oxen walked on, finally stopping in some open green fields where Kentigern buried Fergus and then decided to stay, calling the area the 'dear green place" – 'Glas Gui' or 'Glasgow.'

Kentigern built a chapel and cell, becoming known for his austere lifestyle and his great preaching, and securing many converts. However, a strong anti-Christian movement in the Welsh-lands of Strathclyde forced Kentigern to leave for Wales itself. Time passed and peace came to the Old North of Britain under a new King, Rhydderch Hael who invited Kentigern to return. Kentigern developed his old chapel into a monastery (now the site of Glasgow Cathedral) incorporating the burial site of old Fergus. A community grew as people settled there, drawn once more by his preaching. To this day, Glasgow's full motto is, 'Lord let Glasgow flourish through the preaching of thy word and praising thy name.'

Perhaps wary of his mother's exile, Kentigern never ventured to Lothian and it was St Baldred ('travelling') who earned the title 'Apostle of the Lothians.' His mother was, however, commemorated in Glasgui, becoming a saint in her own right. Over the years, 'Saint Teneu' became corrupted to 'Saint Eneu' then 'Saint Enoch.' She now has a Glasgow underground station named after her, even if most people think St Enoch was male!

Kentigern worked hard, lived an austere life and was an example to others. He drew others to Jesus through the sheer force of his preaching.

Columba (Relational)

> *". . . Come, my children, listen to me; I will teach you the fear of the LORD." (Psalm 34:11)*

Columba was born in Ireland around AD521 and in his early forties he founded the monastery at Iona, and became its first abbot. He died there in AD597, the year that Augustine arrived in England bringing the way of the Church of Rome. We know much of Columba from the 'Life of Columba' written by his cousin Adomnán, a later abbot at Iona with corroboration being found in the Annals of Ulster and the Amra Choluimb Chille.

Columba was implicated in the battle of Cúl Drebene against the High King and under further pressure for having made an unauthorised copy of Finian's manuscript Scripture (possibly the first recorded copyright dispute), he was forced to flee. As we saw, he came to Arran but, Ireland still in sight, continued on – most likely to visit his kinsman, Connall, King of Dál Riata, who granted Columba the island of Iona in AD563.

Columba arrived with 12 other monks, and he led them in maintaining and extending two specific sacraments: Baptism whereby they welcomed new converts into the family of God and Holy Communion or Eucharist (from the Greek for thanksgiving) which continued that family link, that fellowship.

The Iona monastery grew and soon Britons, English, Celts, Irish and even at least one Pict were under holy orders there, in a fellowship that looked to Columba with respect and in fellowship, for he knew them all and related to them all.

Work was hard, both the disciplined lifestyle and the volume of tasks, from farming to building as well as the important pursuits of praying, Bible study and copying Scripture. Columba was with them all, going round each one, interacting with them as they worked, seeing and helping them where they were and receiving and counselling visitors to the island. He was also devoted to studying the Psalms, spending long hours contemplating, transcribing and then discussing with the other monks.

As we have seen, Iona was a centre-point of the Kingdom of Dál Riata, a Thin Place and a seat of learning and theological study. Astride all was the character of Columba, tying the strands together, reaching out to others; much loved. He forged links and kept them: Pictish kings and common folk came to Jesus through Columba's friendship. A colossus in life, he led by serving God; relating to people.

As his life drew to an end, he had a foretelling of when he would die, and spent his last day transcribing from the Psalms which he so loved. Presently he wrote out:

> *"But those who seek the LORD lack no good thing ..." (Psalm 34:10)*

There he ceased, declaring that it would be left, fittingly, to his successor as the leader on Iona to pick up again at the next verse. He went into the monastery itself, lay at the altar and there he died, as Adomnán wrote, "with a countenance full of wonderful joy and gladness."

Adomnán (Protector)

> *My prayer is not that you take them out of the world but that you protect them from the evil one. (John 17:15)*

Adomnán himself was the one who finally persuaded Iona to accept the Roman timing of Easter some years after the Whitby Synod. He was a relative of Columba and became Abbot of Iona in 679. He sought to protect the memory of Columba, writing 'The Life of Saint Columba.' So too he sought to protect the lives of others, writing and promoting the 'Law of the Innocents' designed to guarantee the safety of non-combatants in warfare; an early Geneva Convention.

Aidan (Neighbourliness)

> *He answered, "'Love the Lord your God with all your heart and with all your soul and with all your strength and with all your mind'; and, 'Love your neighbour as yourself.'" "You have answered correctly," Jesus replied. "Do this and you will live." (Luke 10:27-28)*

Aidan was concerned not just *about* travelling, but *how* he travelled. He evangelised as he went with a message of more than just what he did and said, but of who he was in Christ. Aidan was all about sharing with people: property, time and relationship with God; about being a good neighbour.

Aidan's story is caught up in the struggle for the Northumbrian throne. When Edwin became king in 616AD, the princes Oswald and his brother Oswiu went into exile in Iona, where they gained not only an education but were influenced by the Celtic Christian ways. Eventually Oswald secured the throne and eagerly brought Córman as a missionary with him to Northumbria. Córman's strict ways were rejected by the Northumbrians and he returned, despondent, to Iona. It was an Irish monk, Aidan, who suggested that Córman may have been too harsh on the new converts and that he should have "*begun by giving them the milk of simpler teaching, and gradually nourished them with the word of God.*" Invariably, the one who speaks out is the one who gets the job: Aidan was duly consecrated as a bishop and despatched to Northumbria. He met up with King Oswald at Bamburgh and established his missional base 6 miles north at what would become one of Britain's most famous Christian sites: the Holy Island of Lindisfarne.

Aidan brought with him much of what he had learned from Iona – each monk had a soul friend, they read and transcribed the Bible, spent time in contemplation and developed a centre for education. Like Columba, he encouraged praying the Psalms not just as Scripture recitals but as personal prayers.

The Abbot and the King were close, but Aidan demonstrated another neighbourly quality: he visited Oswald when invited and ate frugally. Rarely would he arrive unless asked:

Seldom set foot in your neighbour's house – too much of you, and they will hate you. (Proverbs 25:17)

Oswald (and after his early death in battle, his successor Oswiu) travelled throughout Northumbria with Aidan. These could be long journeys, for Aidan sought to walk everywhere. He would stop and talk to all he met – if they were heathen, he would evangelise and urge them to be baptised; if they were Christian, he would encourage them in their faith. He shared his possessions with those in need: material wealth was not a concern for him. Aidan quite literally talked to people where they were, just as he found them, taking an active interest in their lives and communities.

Irish origins; Scottish influence; English ministry: Aidan has been proposed as a possible patron saint of the United Kingdom (with apologies to the Welsh).

Aidan also founded an abbey at Melrose. Perhaps the most famous monk to have emerged from there was Cuthbert who himself went on to become prior of Lindisfarne.

In demonstrating these neighbourly qualities, Aidan showed not only understanding, but acted out the answer provided by the law expert to Jesus.

Winifred (Healing)

Dear friend, I pray that you may enjoy good health and that all may go well with you, even as your soul is getting along well. (3 John 1:2)

Winifred was born in the early 600s, the daughter of Tyfid ap Eiludd, a Welsh nobleman in South Wales. From early years, she sought a monastic life but being of noble blood (and, by accounts, beautiful), she was sought after as a bride. She favoured holy orders, but one spurned suitor, Caradog, attacked her after she rejected him. Some legends are that he actually beheaded her and she was brought back to life; other accounts are that he slit her throat causing a serious but not fatal injury with lasting scars. Certainly, for the medical standards of the day, her healing was considered miraculous.

Perhaps this healing triggered her godly calling; perhaps it was always her godly gift. But Winifred was healed and then became associated with the healing of others. There was more to her, but there was always the healing. Winifred became known for her wise counsel and administration . . . and her healing abilities. In North Wales, she founded a dual monastery and convent, known first as Winifred's Well and then as Holywell. As its name suggests, it was famous for its healing spring. Winifred is one of the few Celtic saints to have been venerated throughout medieval times and into the present day, and the Holywell shrine is still frequented by pilgrims.

After seven years at Holywell (note the Biblical number for completion), Winifred was guided to Gwytherin in Denbighshire, where she founded and led another convent.

Over the years, only the legends survived and her life story was doubted. However, in 1991, some pieces of a reliquary (a container for relics in a shrine) from the early 8th century were discovered and, from earlier drawings, the pieces were identified as belonging to Winifred, providing some historicity of her.

She is often represented with images representing her wisdom and leadership – usually a crozier (bishop's staff of office) and the wimple of an abbess (not just the 'ordinary' wimple of a nun). But the images also depict the tell-tale scarring at her throat, and the stories told of her always touch on the healing that others experienced.

She died around AD650 at her convent in Gwytherin and was buried there. She was much revered and, in fact, was the patron saint of Wales until her relics were moved to Shrewsbury Abbey in 1138 whereupon the Welsh turned to David, not wanting a saint who was buried in England!

Henry V walked the 50 miles from Shrewsbury to Holywell to give thanks for his victory at Agincourt and to pray for healing – physical, emotional and economic – after the fighting.

It is important to remember that for Winifred, it was not a conveyor belt of physical healing and moving on. The healing was often emotional or spiritual as well. We should acknowledge those who have medical training and godly gifts of healing and at the same time we should ourselves step forward and act, for we help each other by caring for each other's soul needs.

Hild (Leadership)

> *Have confidence in your leaders and submit to their authority, because they keep watch over you as those who must give an account. Do this so that their work will be a joy, not a burden, for that would be of no benefit to you. (Hebrews 13:17)*

We met Hild (or 'Hilda') earlier – one of the wisest, most compassionate and significant of her day. She lived from AD614 to AD680 and, as abbess, she led a community of monks, nuns, lay persons and general workers at Streanæshealh, chairing the Whitby Synod in AD664.

As a girl looking at icons of saints, she was asked if she knew who the saints were. Rather than naming them, she answered generically: "Saints are people who let in the light."

Hild was encouraged by Aidan to set up a community in Northumbria, and she created a double one – for both monks and nuns. She was responsible for faith, well-being and advancement; and for general livelihoods, health and education. Under her leadership, Whitby became a centre for arts and education and for theological study, and Hild saw to it that all people – not just the ordained – could attend and learn.

Bede wrote that, filled with the Holy Spirit and yearning for Jesus, she simply exuded peace and love, which only attracted more people to Whitby under her.

She could find giftings and use them to the Lord's glory. A man, Cædmon, came to work at the monastery, the inference of the records being that he was not then a Christian. Hild sought to engage all people and everyone took a turn singing in entertainment, but Cædmon always slipped away before he was called because he felt he had nothing to offer. One night he dreamt someone appeared and asked him to sing. Cædmon objected that he could not, only to be told, "But you shall sing to me." Cædmon told Hild who set him the task of setting Scripture to poetry and song. He became an ardent evangeliser, and Hilda worked with him in using his poetry and song to reach out to villagers beyond the monastery.

Whitby grew under Hild's leadership and the gospel message flourished under her care. She loved her people and gave of herself for their welfare. She had high standards, using them to measure herself not to condemn others. Her intelligent stewardship of resources allowed her people to live and to live well, providing also for others in charity. And she was always available for counsel, whether as a listening ear or to pronounce and guide; equally so for royalty and ordinary folk. All served her and all loved her, just as she served and loved them.

The Whitby Synod decided against Celtic Christian ways, not against the Bible, so Hild did not run but asked herself: "How do we love Jesus? How do we love each other?" and proceeded to answer those questions through her life and leadership.

Leaders are often said to have a hard edge to them – making them admirable but perhaps not sought out in friendship. Hild displayed a gentleness, nobility and intellectual prowess which made her not just respected as a leader, but loved.

In all her ways, Hild did not just 'let in the light' but she positively reflected out the light that is Jesus.

When Hild died at Whitby, a young nun at Hackness monastery, some 14 miles away, said she saw Hild's soul being borne up by angels and Hackness immediately went into mourning. When a party arrived from Whitby the next day, they were stunned to be told of Hild's death when they themselves were the ones bringing the news.

Cuthbert (Praying)

> *For this reason, since the day we heard about you, we have not stopped praying for you. We continually ask God to fill you with the knowledge of his will through all the wisdom and understanding that the Spirit gives. (Colossians 1:9)*

Cuthbert was born in AD634. Bede wrote much about Cuthbert, for although only fifteen when Cuthbert died, Bede had entered Jarrow monastery aged seven and served alongside an old monk, Sigfrid. Sigfrid had been a novice at Melrose when Cuthbert yielded his horse and spear, entered the church to pray, then approached Prior Boisil seeking holy orders.

A young Cuthbert, as an Anglo-Saxon minor noble, was armed guard for shepherds when on 31st August AD651, in the Lammermuir Hills, he saw a shaft of light. Taking it as both a soul ascending to heaven and godly guidance that he should become a monk, he set off for Melrose, being accepted by Boisil who confirmed that it was Aidan who had died on 31st. Outstanding in study and work, Cuthbert was happiest when simply praying. Under Boisil, he developed a reputation for prayerful contemplation, then travelling on foot and evangelising (much like Aidan).

Abbot Eata, Cuthbert and others established a monastery at Ripon, but after two years they were ousted and forced to return by that ambitious monk Wilfred who, as we saw, would go on win the arguments at the Synod of Whitby and pursue, largely unsuccessfully, high office.

After the Synod of Whitby, Cuthbert became Lindisfarne's prior and set about healing a fractured community. He did so by praying on his own and with those who were on opposing sides, and by listening to them before finally offering his counsel. He meditated on the Lord's Word before mediating on man's word.

Lindisfarne's prior for a decade, he then relinquished office and withdrew to a hermitage on Inner Farne. There he remained, occasionally visited and visiting, but constantly praying. After another decade, he was reluctantly persuaded to become Bishop of Lindisfarne.

Again, Cuthbert governed by prayer and contemplation, by listening and discussing; not by authoritarian decree. Again, he travelled, preached and evangelised. He met to pray with Herbert, his Anam Cara who lived in Cumbria, and who died on the same day as him. After only 2 years as bishop, he returned to Inner Farne where he died in AD687, being buried at Lindisfarne. His body was exhumed on a number of occasions:

AD698 grave 'elevated' into a tomb (undecayed);

AD793 removed inland when Vikings threatened Lindisfarne (undecayed);

(Monks settled on Dunholm (brown hill) as his resting place when they saw a dun cow there, and built a simple church incorporating his tomb.)

1104 church rebuilt, becoming Durham Cathedral (undecayed);

1538 Dissolution of the Monasteries during the Reformation, body reinterred (undecayed);

1827 artefacts removed from the coffin for display (skeleton);

1899 formal post-mortem with findings 'consistent' with all that was known of Cuthbert's life (skeleton).

Given the dun cow and Cuthbert, it is delicious irony that for many years the Edinburgh Co-op was called St Cuthbert's Dairy.

Cuthbert led by prayer; his leadership example was to follow the Holy Spirit and encourage those he met to know and act upon God's will.

> *Then Jesus told him, "Because you have seen me, you have believed; blessed are those who have not seen and yet have believed." (John 20:29)*

9 Provision for the Journey

I had drunk deeply of the Celtic Christian history with the stark dates and bare facts. I had encountered something of them in the context of their time – hearing them calling out to me. I had even seen where they went and what they had – their Thin Places and their tall crosses.

But what did they do that was especially Celtic Christian? Within their culture and within the Faith, what did they leave us so that we could echo their voices?

I could see that the Celtic Christians were led to three key outpourings: in contemplation, in prayer and in blessing. And this equipped and enabled them to provide a powerful expression of Celtic creativity – of poems, epics and hymns.

Celtic Christians, particularly in holy orders, spent time in contemplation and we are all called to this. Dwell on His word. Treasure it in our hearts. The next step, then, would be to contemplate and to allow this to lead me into prayer. We are all called to pray; to enjoy that special communion with God, seeking guidance

and wisdom and even just screaming at God when we cannot see an answer (or at least an answer that we want to have). Above all, prayer allows us to unburden ourselves of worries and burdens and just be open to God,

And this would lead me to blessing. I knew that a blessing shares God's Word, strength and encouragement. I was conscious that that this is of Jesus - not of ourselves. Whether we preface it with "In the name of Jesus, I bless you ..." or dive straight into "May you ..." ultimately, it is simply being connected with God.

And, thus equipped, I could open my ears to the echoes and open my heart to the joyful expression of that connection.

10 Contemplation and Creativity

Celtic Contemplation

I had asked myself how we could contemplate the Lord's glory. I was reminded of a prompting a friend of mine received many years ago when dreams, visons and that quiet inner voice constantly prompted him simply to 'read the Bible.' This led him to create a podcast called the Daily Audio Bible where he reads the Bible fresh each day completed over the year and with insights on each passage. Like Brian, the contemplation of the Celtic Christians would not just be quietly reading the Bible. I am not sure they would have read quietly at all.

Although debated, it seems people in those days rarely read silently. In his book 'Confessions' (written AD 397 – 400), St Augustine noted:

> *But when Ambrose used to read, his eyes were drawn through the pages, while his heart searched for its meaning; however, his voice and tongue were quiet. Often when we were present – for anyone could approach him and it was not his habit that visitors be announced to him – we saw him reading in this fashion, silently and never otherwise.*

Perhaps Augustine was annoyed with Ambrose for continuing to read (as we might be today when talking to someone who continues texting), but it seems that reading silently was remarkable to him. Of course, there were earlier instances, but clearly as exceptions: Plutarch recorded the confusion of the watching soldiers when Alexander the Great (in the 4th century BC) silently read a letter from his mother.

Most people were illiterate and those who could read would do so aloud. Individual words were neither separated nor punctuated, but instead itallrantogetherasone making it much more difficult to read silently. It seems only in the tenth century that silent reading became standard.

With the monks and nuns generally literate, but without photocopiers or printing presses, to them fell the holy task of copying Scripture and creating new Bibles. Here was time for contemplation. Every activity could be an act of worship and transcribing would be dwelt on, not just finished quickly. As they worked, they would study, pray and just 'think' about what they were copying out. In this way, they created gloriously intricate and colourful Bibles – intended for reading and studying, not for display cases.

We do not actually need silence or anything else. We just to give ourselves up to God, finding a regularity and rhythm as the Celtic Christians did and, after all, Luke recorded Jesus going to the Mount of Olives to pray "as usual." (Luke 22:39)

Contemplation is not just emptying your mind of distraction, but positively inviting the Holy Spirit to fill you. It's not the technique that matters, it's choosing God. A good friend of mine wrote a book called Praying for your Elephant: List your prayer requests and then, and this is the cunning part, put away the list and concentrate on your relationship with God. Later, dig out the list and see how many have been answered.

Celtic Prayers

Like us, Celtic Christians were called to pray without ceasing. Praying is connecting with God and like us, they were called to live in God's presence, not focussing on grand prayer techniques.

They prayed into any occasion. Nothing was their own power, effort or entitlement, not even simply getting up in the morning:

I arise today
Through the power of Christ's birth with his baptism,
Through the power of his crucifixion with his burial,
Through the power of his resurrection with his ascension.

Celtic Christian prayers were real . . . immediate . . . and just the same as ours. Perhaps they just had the rhythm of God in their prayer life.

Almost as with French grammar, Celtic Christians would pray in the avoir (to have) and the être (to be). They would call on the Lord to "Bestow upon us fullness in our need" and would invite Him to "Be my soul in the trustance of the High King." They looked for protection, through lorica (armour) and caim (encircling) prayers.

Lorica prayer sought God's protection in all aspects of life. This was Ephesians 6:10-20 stuff; the full armour, through God's grace and love.

Father cherish me; Son cherish me; Spirit cherish me. Three all-kindly.

Three aid my hope; Three aid my love; Three aid my eye

And my knee from stumbling.

Caim prayer sought God's protection in a deliberate act of encircling, inspired by Joshua and by God's powerful love surrounding us:

On the seventh day, they got up at daybreak and marched around the city seven times in the same manner, except that on that day they circled the city seven times. (Joshua 6:15)

As the mountains surround Jerusalem, so the Lord surrounds his people both now and forevermore. (Psalm 125:2)

Caim is not powerfully encircling ourselves; it is giving ourselves up to Jesus' power. At the centre – always – is Jesus, then as now.

Christ with me,
Christ before me,
Christ behind me,
Christ within me,
Christ beneath me,
Christ above me,
Christ at my right,
Christ at my left,
Christ when I lie down,
Christ when I sit down,
Christ when I stand.

Christ in the heart of everyone who thinks of me,
Christ in the mouth of everyone who speaks to me,
Christ in the eye of everyone who sees me,
Christ in the ear of everyone who hears me.

Celtic Blessings

A blessing is just a prayer. But if *Lorica* and *Chaim* prayers were the Celtic Christians seeking God's protection for themselves and others, then blessings were an outpouring of the power of prayer and of their relationship with God.

In the Old Testament there was the priestly blessing:

The Lord bless you and keep you;
the Lord make his face shine on you
and be gracious to you;
the Lord turn his face toward you
and give you peace. (Numbers 6: 24-26)

Similarly, the Celtic Christians blessed each other:

And the King of kings,
and Jesus Christ
and the Spirit of peace
and of grace will be with us;
of grace will be with us.

Consider what we often simply call 'THE grace':

May the grace of the Lord Jesus Christ, and the love of God, and the fellowship of the Holy Spirit be with you all. (2 Corinthians 13:14)

And then let it take shape in the context of the Celtic Christian world:

May the King shield you in the valleys,
May Christ aid you on the mountains,
May Spirit bathe you on the slopes,
in hollow, on hill, on plain,
Mountain, valley and plain.

Celtic Christians took their learning from the Bible and applied it to their own context and surroundings. Celtic Christianity is not just one topic (in this instance, blessing), and so we must also look outwards and beyond: to their relationship with the world. They blessed each other and the world because they recognised God's authority over everyone, every place, every thing. This can inspire us to be more aware of the people we encounter, the countryside available to us and even the city surrounding us.

Or consider communion (the Eucharist) where we 'share the peace.' For us, this is usually a handshake or a kiss with the words "the peace of Christ." For the Celtic Christians, it would be prefaced by a prayer-talk with God, a prayer-blessing for others and then actually sharing that peace. Maybe you can pray-talk this at communion:

Peace between neighbours
Peace between kindred,
Peace between lovers,
In love of the King of life.
Peace between person and person,
Peace between wife and husband,
Peace between woman and children,
The peace of Christ above all peace.
Bless, O Christ, my face,
Let my face bless every thing;
Bless, O Christ, mine eye,
Let mine eye bless all it sees.

And having prayed that blessing, THEN share it by offering the handshake, the holy kiss and 'the peace of Christ.'

You will be blessed in the city and blessed in the country. (Deuteronomy 28:3)

Celtic Creativity

The Celtic Christians had a strong oral tradition of poetry and prayer. They were handed down, spoken and sung; repeated and learned.

Celtic Christians had a particular expression of their love of God, reverence of the Holy Spirit and delight in Jesus. The oft-repeated words were embedded in the memories of the individual and the community. They prepared themselves for worship using the natural rhythms of God's creation all around them (the ebb and flow of the waves, the rise and fall of a light breeze, the percussion of a river dashing over rocks), alongside which they might repeat:

I am bending my knee
In the eye of the Father who created me,
In the eye of the Son who purchased me,
In the eye of the Spirit who cleansed me,
In friendship and affection.
(Carmina Gadelica Vol 1)

But that oral tradition was not the only medium for Celtic Christians. Scripture was written out and its meaning and beauty contemplated.

Copies of the Bible were laboriously and lovingly prepared often at vast religious settlements such as Iona, under Columba, and Whitby, led by Hild. An entire community was built around God's Word, copying it out to share it and evangelise.

The ground was fertile: crops to feed the body. The culture was fertile: the arts to nurture soul and spirit. Hymns, poems and epic tales all pointed to God's glory. Expressing faith was not just preaching a sermon but connecting in different ways.

Cædmon the Whitby herdsman was encouraged by Hild (Anglo-Saxon, but of the Celtic Christian tradition) to compose and sing out his poetry, all in praise of the one in his dream all in praise of Jesus. And wonderfully, Cædmon wrote of the Creator God providing '*Thā middungeard moncynnæs uard*' ('the middle earth as their land') – '*middungeard*' means 'middle earth' so clearly Tolkien was onto something!

> *. . . be filled with the Spirit, speaking to one another with psalms, hymns, and songs from the Spirit. Sing and make music from your heart to the Lord . . .* (Ephesians 5: 18-19)

11 The Journey Continues (Go and Do Likewise)

I have come a long way. I am not there yet, but I am comfortable on my journey; I know the path I am on, although I do need help to stay on that path and not wander.

I have looked at the history of the Celtic Christians, and found they are not much different from us.

I have considered – and been to – some of the Thin Places, and begun to understand what it is to meet with God. I see that we do not *need* the Thin Places, but that they are beautiful and enhancing when we are there.

I have found the importance of prayer, and that that the best way to learn to pray is simply to pray. I have seen that prayer is not just protection from evil for others; it is positively blessing others in the name of Jesus and I have seen that it is good to pray for ourselves. That is not selfish; it is simply continuing our conversation with and reliance on Father God. And it is good to have a routine, a structure, in our prayer life but we must recognise that prayer is appropriate at any time and at every time.

I have seen how attributes of the saints (and we are all saints) builds up a more complete picture of Jesus. He truly is our everything.

And I have revelled in the creativity of the Celtic Christians – in their poetry and in their general writing and singing.

I have so much still to learn. But how have I got this far and how can I go on? Quite simply by listening, I have listened to the Celtic Christians of old as they speak down the centuries.

In doing so, I have found myself drawn a little bit closer to Jesus, grown a wee bit more accustomed to the Holy Spirit, drawn closer under the protection of Father God.

It may be faint in places (and loud in the Thin Places) but if you settle and listen, you can still hear them – it – calling out to you today. It begins with an echo of a theme and a feature and then it builds, sweeping you away and drawing you close as you chase the Wild Goose and grow closer to God. Listen to the echoes of Celtic Christianity, and hear them as they point to the way to the eternal Lord.

We have come a long way since we first caught a glimpse of the Celtic Christians. Hopefully we have seen that we are all essentially the same. We are human beings in need of God who not only created us, but who sustains us – for He provides life, justice and mercy through His love and power.

In the Celtic Christians, we have seen how different peoples can not only see themselves as family, but *be* family; not through ourselves, but through being adopted by God the Father.

It can be good to find quiet times and quiet places – not as ends in themselves, but as a means of shedding distractions and drawing closer to God. He is always here: do we choose to turn to face Him or to turn away from Him?

We have seen how fulfilling a good and godly life is when we simply get on with it. But we need to remember that getting on with life includes times of contemplation – are we actually doing as God calls us; using the giftings God has given us. Are we actively supporting others or just helping ourselves?

We were created to be in relationship, fellowship, community. We can come together and hold ourselves accountable to each other and to an especial dear one whom God provides for that purpose – and through all that, we can draw closer to God.

We can admire and learn from godly traits in others, but as a means of inspiring us to do godly things ourselves. We do not need to travel to journey; we do not need to see the result for there to be completion of God's will.

We can learn and follow the importance of timing – seasons of activity and of rest.

We can relax into the care and love which our Father has for us all, through the power of a blessing:

The blessing of God and the Lord be yours.
The blessing of the perfect Spirit be yours,
The blessing of the Three be pouring for you
Mildly and generously, Mildly and generously.

We can seek protection in prayer, noting that God (Father, Son and Holy Spirit) provides us with the means of our protection even as we seek Him to encircle and surround us in providing for us and in loving us:

Form of Christ before thee
Form of God behind thee
Stream of Spirit through thee
To succour and aid thee.

We have blessings, caim and lorica prayers, in Psalms:

Surely, Lord, you bless the righteous;
you surround them with your favour
as with a shield. (Psalm 5:12)

We are called to walk in step with Jesus so that we can see what he sees, do what he does, rest when he rests.

The Celtic Christians found so much expression and inspiration in simplicity, in prayer and in just looking to Jesus. But the point is not to stop there, admiring them. The point is to recognise – and to do – what Jesus asks of us, and so it is appropriate to close with that famous line from Luke:

'Go and do likewise.' (Luke 10:37)

You used to walk in these ways, in the life you once lived. (Colossians 3:7)

12 Acknowledgements

I have read many books on Celtic Christianity as I journeyed back to hear for myself the echoes of who they were. Whether in part or in whole, and whether intentionally or by osmosis, I have learned from all of them. Some resonated with me and clearly influenced me, as I embraced their rhythms and interpretations. I list the main books here, acknowledging the fine research and writing by authors which made my own amateur attempts both easy and pleasurable. I hope this list encourages you to delve further into this fascinating culture.

Aiden, Bede, Cuthbert: Three Inspirational Saints by David Adam (SPCK Publishing)

A Staff to the Pilgrim by Gabriel Cooper Rochelle (Golden Alley Press)

Carmina Gadelica by Alexander Carmichael (Internet Archive) (the prayers and blessings are taken from this collection)

Celtic Advent by David Cole (BRF)

Celtic Journeys in Scotland and the North of England by Shirley Toulson (Fount)

Celtic Lent by David Cole (BRF)

Celtic Prayers and Practices by David Cole (BRF)

Celtic Saints by David Cole (BRF)

Celtic Saints in their Landscape by Elizabeth Rees (Amberley Publishing)

Celtic Year by David Cole (BRF)

Columba's Iona: A new History by Rosalind K. Marshall (Sandstone Press)

Cuthbert of Farne by Katherine Tiernan (Sacristy Press)

Every Earthly Blessing: Rediscovering the Celtic Tradition by Esther de Waal (Morehouse Publishing)

Hilda of Whitby by Ray Simpson (BRF)

Life of St Columba by Admonán of Iona translated by Richard Sharpe (Penguin Classics)

Restoring the Woven Cord by Michael Mitton (BRF)

Saint Andrew: Scotland's Myth and Identity by Michael TRB Turnbull (Saint Andrew Press)

The Celtic Saints by Nigel Pennick (Thorsons)

Thin Places: An Evangelical Journey into Celtic Christianity by Tracy Balzer (Leafwood Publishers)

All Scripture quotations are from The NIV translation of the Bible apart from *The Passion Transation* in section 6.